'Know the Game' Series

# *Archery*
## *by Tom Foy*

# contents

GW00357474

*Printed in Great Britain by*
*Jowett & Sowry Ltd. Leeds*

# Foreword

I am delighted to write this foreword to yet another edition of 'Know the Game—Archery' because it is obvious that a great many copies of the previous editions have been bought by people who were interested in discovering more about Archery.

Archery has advantages over lots of other sports because age is no barrier, you are never too young, nor too old, to take up archery, neither do physical handicaps debar anyone from enjoying the sport as witness the many archery clubs for disabled archers throughout the country.

The reasons for the growth of archery are many and varied but apart from the fact that the British appear to have an inborn love for bows and arrows, it is without doubt a true family sport and one in which every member of the family can participate with equal enjoyment.

The most popular form of the sport is target archery in which personal scores are always recorded with the result that an archer shoots against his own best score and also against known record scores. There are of course many other forms of archery including flight shooting, field archery, clout shooting, archery golf and archery darts, details of which can be found in this excellent little book.

Today the sport of archery continues to grow and flourish not only in Britain but also in many countries throughout the world and so the strength and appeal of this sport has now resulted in the introduction of Archery into the Olympic Games at Munich in 1972.

*Eric W. Strickland*

*Eric W. Strickland*
*President, The Grand National Archery Society*

The Society will be staging the XXVIth World Championship in Target Archery in the City of York in 1971.

# Introduction

The first two questions that people ask when they are thinking of taking up archery are 'How much will it cost?' and 'Do you think that I could become any good at it?' The first question is easy to answer, for an adult beginner can purchase all of his equipment for under seven pounds. This equipment will be fairly basic but quite adequate for taking up the sport, and a new archer can become quite skilful with it before he goes on to more expensive items. At the very beginning it may not even be necessary to buy equipment, for most clubs keep a small amount of equipment for beginners to use before they make up their minds to buy their own.

The second question is almost impossible to answer, for there seems to be no way of telling whether a person will eventually be capable of high scores or not. It is certain that an archer's physique has little relation to his ability, so it can be safely assumed that good shooting is achieved by really thinking about it and concentrating on practice.

This book alone cannot make you a skilful archer; no book can, but it can put you on the right road by showing you the basic points of good shooting on which you can build with practice and concentration, and we hope that it will give you that final push to start you shooting. It tells you quite a lot about the sport so that when you do make your first visit to a club you will understand what everyone is talking about and doing and what all the unfamiliar terms mean.

Fig. 1. *English longbowmen versus French crossbowmen at the Battle of Crecy during 100 years war.*

One thing is certain; if you have bought this book (or if you have read this far in the shop), then you have got that basic interest in the sport that has made archers out of thousands of people in all walks of life. Why not make up your mind to 'have a go' right now in this fascinating and friendly sport of archery. Whether you become a champion or stay a 'beginner', you will enjoy every minute of it.

# How do I start?

Without a doubt, the first thing to do is to find your nearest club, for clubs are the backbone of archery. It should not be too difficult, for local sports-shops usually know. Failing that try the library or call at the local newspaper office; they will almost certainly be in touch with all local organisations. If this should fail then write to your Regional Secretary, whose address you will find in the Appendix at the end of this book.

Once you have found a club, you will find many new friends, and they will all be happy to help you. It is likely that the club will have its own instructor, or even a qualified coach, and he will tell you what equipment to buy. Archery tackle is as individual as a suit, so never buy equipment before going to a club, for beginners who buy equipment without getting expert advice almost always get the wrong size, and it is a great pity to be put off the sport right at the start simply because of incorrect equipment.

Except for clubs which are financed by firms for their employees, almost all clubs are self-supporting, so you will be expected to pay an annual membership fee. This will vary according to the size of the club and what its annual expenses are, but the average membership fee is probably in the region of three guineas. This entitles you to a number of things, but the most important ones at this stage are the use of the club's targets and ground. Most clubs hold a few beginners' bows and arrows and are only too pleased to let anyone use them for a few weeks. However, as soon as a beginner decides that he wants to go ahead and become a member of the club, he will be expected to purchase his own equipment.

# What equipment will I need?

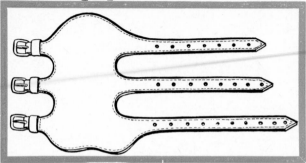

Fig. 2. *The bracer.*

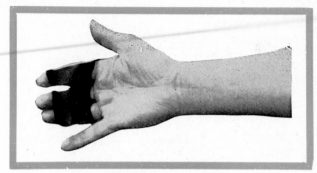

Fig. 3. *The tab in use.*

Obviously you must have a bow and some arrows, but there are two other important items of equipment, a bracer and a tab, and we will talk about these first. The bracer (Fig. 2) is made of tough leather, and its other name, the armguard, will tell you what it is for. It is strapped to the inside of the forearm of the hand holding the bow, and it protects the arm from any chance blows that might be inflicted by the string when the bow is shot. The string should not really hit the arm at all, but a badly made shot might cause it to do so; it is therefore essential to wear a bracer, especially in your early days of shooting.

The tab (Fig. 3) is a specially shaped piece of leather which goes on to the fingers of the hand which will draw the string back. The first and third fingers go through the two holes, and the second finger goes into the gap between the holes. The tab now rests flat on the inside of the fingers, with the rough side next to the skin, and the narrow slit in the tab should be between the first and second fingers. Archers never pull the arrow back, they pull the string back and let the arrow come with it, and this tab is used to prevent the string from making the fingers sore with the abrasion from each shot. The illustration will make this clear. When choosing a tab, get one that is shiny, and does not overlap the fingers too much. It may have to be cut down a little, but get advice before you do this.

Having obtained these two small but important items we can proceed with the other essential ones, the bow and the arrows. With the help of your club instructor you have now to find out what weight of bow and what length of arrow you need. Incidentally, when archers talk about the 'weight' of a bow, they mean how much it takes to pull it back to its full extent, not how much it would weigh on a scale, which is called the 'weight-in-hand'. As well as being available in a variety of weights, bows are available in different sizes, and this is determined by the length of arrow to be used, so before anything else, a new archer must find his proper arrow length, or 'draw-length'.

This draw-length is decided by each archer's length of arm and breadth of shoulder. An easy way of discovering your draw-length is to stretch out your arms in front of you, and hold an arrow between your finger-tips with the end of the arrow resting on your chest, level with your shoulders (Fig. 4). If the arrow you are using is the correct length for you, it should project about an inch past your finger-tips. If there is any doubt in your mind about which of two lengths to use, then choose the longer, even if it means that when shooting you do not draw the arrows right to the point. A short arrow can be dangerous, for the archer may pull it back too far and the point will then come inside the bow. Remember that it is often possible to shorten your arrows later on, but you cannot lengthen them.

Arrows are normally purchased in sets of eight, six for regular shooting and two for spares in case of damage. The cheapest arrows are made of wood, but if you can

Fig. 4. *Finding the correct arrow length.*

afford to pay a little more, then it is better to buy arrows made of aluminium. These are much less liable to break and are more accurate than wooden ones, so are a better buy in the long run. It is also possible to straighten an aluminium arrow which has accidentally become bent, but it is not possible to straighten a wooden arrow.

Now that the draw-length has been found and the arrows chosen, a suitable bow must be found. The cheapest bow is a flat bow made of lemonwood, but just because it is cheap it does not mean that it is unsuitable for learning to shoot well; in fact it is ideal for the first months of shooting. There are bows available made of solid glass-fibre which are a little more expensive, and

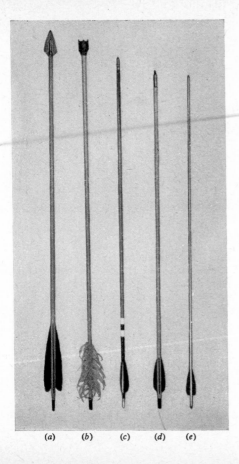

(a)    (b)    (c)    (d)    (e)

Fig. 5. Left to right:

(a) *Hunting arrow with a broadhead point and a large fletchings. These big fletchings are needed to keep the arrow on a straight flight, for if the ordinary size fletchings were used the large flat broadhead would make the arrow veer off course.*

*There is not a great deal of hunting done in Britain, but it is very popular in the United States; some States even set aside certain weeks for bow hunting before the gun season starts.*

(b) *Fru-fru arrow with a blunt fitted. These arrows would be used for shooting upwards, for instance at something in a tree. The blunt gives a hard blow without sticking in, allowing the arrow to return to earth, and the fru-fru has so much drag in the air that it comes down safely at a very low speed. It is the only type of arrow that should ever be shot into the air because of the great danger involved in the high speeds of other types. It is more a 'novelty' arrow than anything else.*

(c) *Wooden target arrow with a hardwood foot. Such arrows are used by archers who want as accurate and strong an arrow as possible without departing from traditional materials. They should not be confused with beginners' wooden arrows, which are not footed.*

(d) *Field arrow made of wood and fitted with a field pile. Because of the rough country used for field-shooting, arrows are easily lost, so the majority of archers use wooden arrows because of their low price. The more expert archers use arrows made from glass-fibre, which are extremely strong, but expensive.*

(e) *Target arrow made from high strength aluminium alloy. Over 90 per cent. of all the arrows used in this country are of this type. The price for a set of eight varies from £2 to £10, depending on their strength, accuracy, and quality of finish, so there are arrows of this type to suit every pocket and every standard of archer. Some archers prefer their target arrows to be fletched with plastic instead of the usual turkey feathers because they stand up to rain better, but experience is needed to shoot them successfully.*

7

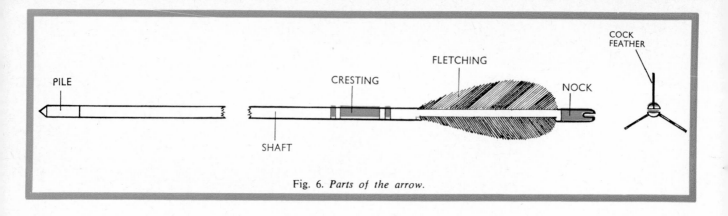

Fig. 6. *Parts of the arrow.*

these also are recommended for the beginner. Do not, at this stage, go in for one of the steel or composite bows, which are much more expensive and would be a waste of money to you so early in your shooting. Whilst you are shooting with one of the cheap bows you will be developing a good style and learning things about your own shooting which will allow you to choose exactly the right bow when you have become skilful enough to warrant buying a more expensive one.

Whichever bow you purchase, it is most important that it is light enough for you to handle easily. Do not forget that there is a great deal of difference between drawing a bow two or three times in a shop and shooting with it all day, and in the early stages of learning to shoot you will have to stand with the bow fully drawn for several seconds while various faults in the way you are holding and aiming are corrected. Because people vary so much in strength it is not possible to give definite weights to buy, but a rough guide is from 30 to 35 pounds for men and 20 to 25 pounds for ladies. Be modest in your estimate of your own strength, for it is true to say that a person with a bow that is far too weak can learn to shoot well with it, but a person with a bow that is too heavy may never learn to shoot at all.

Although the basic equipment is all you need to start with, there are a few other items which you will find

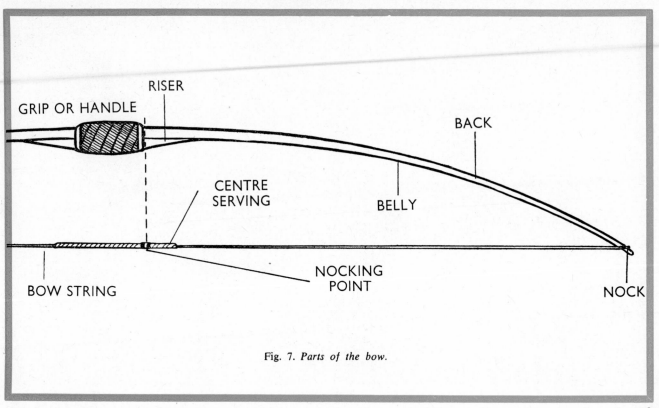

RISER

GRIP OR HANDLE

BACK

CENTRE
SERVING

BELLY

NOCKING
POINT

BOW STRING

NOCK

Fig. 7. *Parts of the bow.*

Fig. 8. *Ground quiver in use holding bow and spare arrows.*

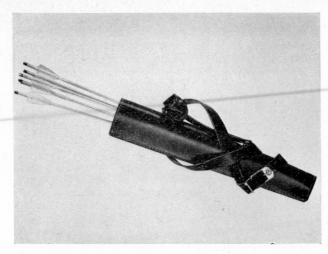

Fig. 9. *Quiver with waist-belt.*

leaving your bow on while you walk to the target. Both of these types of quiver are not difficult to make once you have seen them, and in fact most of the marvellous-looking quivers which appear at tournaments are home made.

A large woollen tassel can be made easily at home; this is hung from the belt along with the quiver and is used to wipe earth from arrows which have missed the target and hit the ground. You will use this quite frequently to start with! It is a good idea to buy a score-pad now, for if you start to keep your scores as soon as you start hitting the target you will find it encouraging to see your scores improving from week to week.

# What should I wear?

The accepted colours for archery are dark green and white, so if you already have any casual clothing in these colours, then wear this. At the National Championships these colours must be worn, but in your club anything casual will do and the matter of the correct colours can be left until some future time when you are choosing new clothes. It is most important that either short sleeves are worn or that clothing on the arms is tight, for anything loose on the arms is certain to get caught in the bow-string and spoil your shooting. It is advisable to have stout footwear to keep out damp on wet grass.

useful. First of all there is the quiver (Fig. 9), which holds the arrows for you conveniently to hand. This hangs from a belt around your waist (not over the shoulder; that is a hunting-quiver).

Another item you will find a great help is a ground-quiver (Fig. 8). This is made of metal, and it is really just a stand that is pushed into the ground well behind the shooting-line, and it is for your spare arrows and for

# Stringing the bow

You will see that your bow-string is looped around the bow at one end and tied on with a timber-hitch at the other. The end with the knot is the bottom of the bow, and this is put against the instep of the left foot (Fig. 10). Grasp the handle with the left hand, and hold the bow so that the string is away from you; in other words, the bow is between you and the string. Place the heel of the right hand on the top limb, with the thumb and forefinger on the sides of the limb just below the loop. Now pull with the left hand and push with the right, and let the right hand slide slowly up the limb taking the loop with it. As the loop slides up the top limb guide it into the nocks, but before you relax the pressure make sure that the loop is well and truly in the nocks and is not going to come out as soon as you let go.

The illustration should make this clear, but if you find it difficult, these are the things to check. Firstly, keep your right thumb and forefinger at the sides of the limb and you will not run the risk of getting your fingers caught between the bow and the string. Secondly, make sure that your left hand is doing its fair share of the work and is not letting your right hand push it away from you;

Fig. 10. *Stringing a wooden bow.*

and finally, it is only the heel of the right hand which does any pushing, not the palm or fingers.

Your bow is now braced, or strung, but there are two further jobs to be done before shooting; putting on a nocking-point, and fixing a sight or aiming-mark. Put an arrow on the string at the point where it makes a right angle with the string when it is resting on the arrow shelf, and then move the arrow up the string by one eighth of an inch. With some linen thread (or preferably dental-floss from a chemist) bind around the string either side of the arrow (Fig. 11); not a lot, just enough to prevent the arrow from sliding up or down. Every arrow will now be shot from exactly the same place on the string, and this will make for greater accuracy.

To fix a sight, measure the distance between your aiming eye and the underside of the chin, and then mark the inside of the upper limb of the bow the same height above the arrow rest. A simple pencil mark will do, or a thin strip of sticky tape.

Put on your bracer and tab, buckle on your quiver of arrows, and you are now ready to shoot.

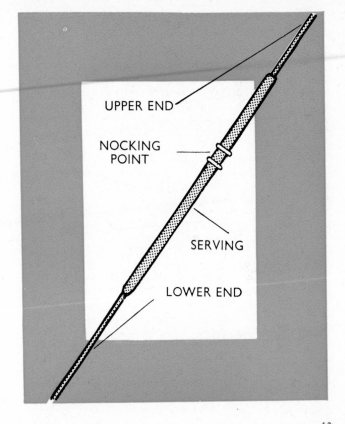

UPPER END

NOCKING POINT

SERVING

LOWER END

Fig. 11. *Diagram of parts of serving.*

# The right way to shoot

Archers work on the reasonable assumption that if every arrow in a perfect set is shot in exactly the same way they will all fall in exactly the same spot, so they try to achieve a style in every part of their shooting that they can repeat over and over again without variation. You have seen the application of this idea in putting a nocking point on the string, so that the arrows are shot from the same spot every time.

Start by finding out which is your controlling eye. If you are right-handed, you will normally hold the bow in your left hand and aim with your right eye, but in some people the left eye is the stronger, or controlling eye, and this will try to take over the aiming. To find out which is your controlling eye, point quickly at an object a few yards away, with both eyes open. Keep your finger still and close your left eye. If your finger remains on the object your governing eye is the right, but if your finger appeared to jump to the left when you shut your left eye, then the left is the controlling one.

If this is so in your case, then you have the choice of holding the bow in the other hand, or of keeping the left eye closed during aiming. Some people do not have a controlling eye and are able to please themselves which hand they hold the bow in, but they have to shoot with one eye closed. It is worth while spending some time on deciding which way you want to shoot, for although beginners' bows can be shot in either hand, the more expensive composite bows are made for either one hand

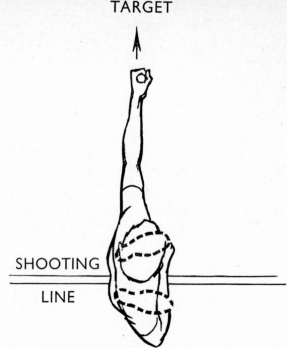

Fig. 12. *Position on line.*

or the other, so that you must buy a new bow if you want to change over.

For describing the actions of shooting we shall assume that you are in fact going to hold the bow in the left hand. Stand astride the shooting line with your left side

Fig. 13. *The bow arm is nearly straight but not rigid. The elbow is not locked. Wooden bow in use.*

Fig. 14. *The grip on the bow. Glass-fibre bow in use.*

towards the target (Fig. 12). Do not face the target, but stand at right angles to it so that your shoulder points towards it, and stand with your feet apart for better balance, just enough to be comfortable: and do not move them again until you have finished shooting each arrow (our 'same every time' theory again).

The bow should be held gently, not tightly, and in such a position that the pull of the bow is taken in a straight line down the forearm (Fig. 13). The wrist should be dropped slightly so that the weight is spread over the pad at the base of the thumb (Fig. 14) instead of all being taken by the fork between the thumb and forefinger.

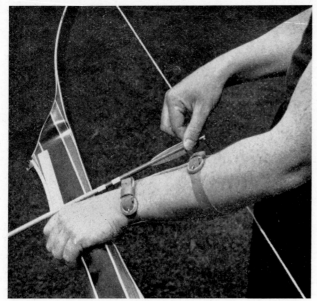

Fig. 15. *Nocking the arrow. Modern composite bow in use.*

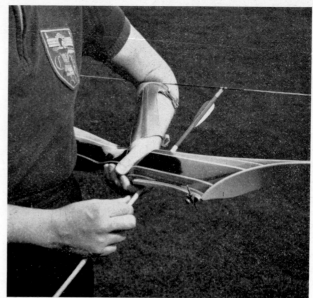

Fig. 16. *Alternative method favoured by some archers.*

When you are happy with your grip on the bow, bring the bow horizontally in front of your body, at waist height; with your right hand lay an arrow on the bow at the arrow rest, and then push the nock of the arrow on to the nocking point with the cockfeather (the odd-coloured one) pointing upwards (Fig. 15), away from the bow. The arrow should not fit too tightly on the string, for this will make it squeeze itself off; nor should it be so loose that it falls off again, but it should grip just enough to hold on whilst the string is pulled back.

The work of pulling the string is done by three fingers of the right hand, the forefinger above the arrow, and the second and third fingers underneath the arrow. The string should lie in the first crease of all three fingers and the joints should be bent just enough to hold the string but no more; the little finger should hang loosely but must not be curled up into the palm. The first and second fingers should not actually touch the arrow for there should be a gap of about one-eighth of an inch either side. Leaving this gap before you draw will prevent the string from squeezing or 'pinching' the fingers against the arrow as you draw back. Take up a little of the weight, and see that only the first joints are bending. The back of the hand, the wrist, and the forearm should be absolutely flat and in line with the arrow (Fig. 17).

Before drawing the bow, stand erect, turn your head towards the target (Fig. 18), and look at the target throughout the draw. It is important not to look down at your equipment whilst you are drawing. The bow should be drawn by pushing with your left hand whilst pulling with your right hand, and turning the bow into the upright position at the same time. The work should be shared equally between both arms, but only the arms, for the body should remain still throughout the draw. At the end of the draw (Fig. 19) the string should be touching the middle of the chin and the tip of the nose, and the edge of the forefinger should be in contact with the underside of the chin. This position is known as the 'anchor' (Figs. 20 and 21).

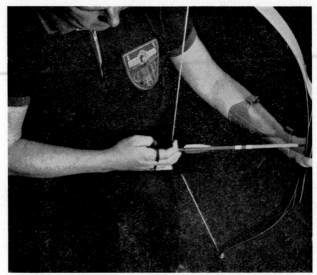

Fig. 17. *During the draw it is essential that the back of the hand remains flat.*

Many beginners find that as they draw the string back the arrow falls off the rest, but this can be easily cured once they know the reason. As they feel the weight increasing during the draw there is a tendency for them to curl the fingers more tightly in case the string should slip off. This extra curling twists the string around, and this twist is imparted to the arrow, which then falls off

Fig. 18. *Look at the target, not the equipment during the draw.*

Fig. 19. *The completion of the draw.*

the rest. So the answer is simply to make sure that the fingers are sufficiently far on the string at the beginning to make it unnecessary to tighten the grip later in the draw.

It is worth while spending plenty of time in practising the draw without shooting, until you can get a really good 'anchor' straight away, with the string pulled hard into the centre of the chin, and with no gap between the forefinger and the underside of the chin. Do make sure that it is your hand that brings the string to the chin, and

Fig. 20. *A good 'anchor'.*

Fig. 21. *Back view of 'anchor'.*

not your chin that goes forward to meet the string. The bow-arm should be nearly straight, but not rigid, so that the hollow part of the arm faces inwards rather than the bones of the elbow. This will prevent bruises from the bowstring which can be received when the elbow is locked.

Once you are able to come to full draw easily and steadily, and are able to get a good anchor, you are ready to start aiming. No matter what distance you are shooting from, the aiming eye should always be focused on the target, not the bow or the sight. The aiming mark

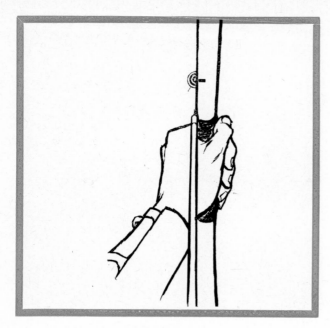

Fig. 22. *Aiming.*

Fig. 23. *After the loose. Keep still until the arrow has struck.*

you have put on the bow is suitable for approximately twenty yards, and this is the best distance at which to start shooting. When at full draw the left hand edge of the bow should be in line with the centre of the target, and by moving slightly at the waist the bow can be lowered or raised in order to get the aiming mark on the bow level with the gold (Fig. 22).

Now pause! The few seconds between aiming and loosing are one of the most important points of shooting, for they should be used to ask yourself such questions as

'Am I perfectly steady, is the string pressed against my chin or has it crept away, am I pinching the arrow, is the back of my right hand in a straight line with my wrist?' The list of possible questions is endless and will vary from one archer to another, but even if you are certain that everything is exactly right there must still be a pause between aiming at the gold and loosing the arrow. Archers who get into the habit of loosing as soon as they get their aiming mark on the gold find, after a while, that as soon as their sight appears on the gold they loose automatically and uncontrollably, even though they were not really ready; the arrow seems to go off on its own. It sounds very odd, but it does happen, so do pause before you loose. The real **you** must decide when to loose, not some annoying reflex action.

The loose is probably the most critical point of shooting, for if it is badly done all the effort put into your anchor and aiming will be wasted. The arrow should not be loosed simply by opening the fingers; instead, try to pull the string more tightly into the chin so that the slight backward movement of the hand pulls the string off the fingers. Apart from this slight backward movement of the drawing hand, you should remain perfectly still and look at the gold until the arrow has hit the target (Fig. 23). If you find after shooting several arrows that you are consistently shooting too high, then raise the bowsight a little, and vice-versa. Although it will be some time before you can get all your arrows in the gold at this distance, you should try, by altering your sight, to get the gold in the centre of the pattern your arrows make.

# What are 'Rounds'?

Archers shoot a set number of arrows at set distances, and these combinations are known as 'Rounds'. Here are the main ones we shoot in Britain.

**York**
72 arrows at 100 yards.
48 arrows at 80 yards.
24 arrows at 60 yards.

**Hereford**
72 arrows at 80 yards.
48 arrows at 60 yards.
24 arrows at 50 yards.

**St. George**
36 arrows at 100 yards.
36 arrows at 80 yards.
36 arrows at 60 yards.

**Albion**
36 arrows at 80 yards.
36 arrows at 60 yards.
36 arrows at 50 yards.

**Long Western**
48 arrows at 80 yards.
48 arrows at 60 yards.

**Western**
48 arrows at 60 yards.
48 arrows at 50 yards.

**Long National**
48 arrows at 80 yards.
24 arrows at 60 yards.

**National**
48 arrows at 60 yards.
24 arrows at 50 yards.

**Windsor**
36 arrows at 60 yards.
36 arrows at 50 yards.
36 arrows at 40 yards.

**American**
30 arrows at 60 yards.
30 arrows at 50 yards.
30 arrows at 40 yards.

**F.I.T.A. (Gentlemen)**
36 arrows at 90 metres.
36 arrows at 70 metres.
36 arrows at 50 metres.
36 arrows at 30 metres.

**F.I.T.A. (Ladies)**
36 arrows at 70 metres.
36 arrows at 60 metres.
36 arrows at 50 metres.
36 arrows at 30 metres.

## Junior Rounds

*Bristol I*
72 arrows at 80 yards.
48 arrows at 60 yards.
24 arrows at 50 yards.

*Bristol II*
72 arrows at 60 yards.
48 arrows at 50 yards.
24 arrows at 40 yards.

*Bristol III*
72 arrows at 50 yards.
48 arrows at 40 yards.
24 arrows at 30 yards.

*Bristol IV*
72 arrows at 40 yards.
48 arrows at 30 yards.
24 arrows at 20 yards.

In all these rounds the longest distance is shot first and the shortest last, and except for the F.I.T.A., the standard four-foot target is used. In the F.I.T.A. Round at 90, 70, and 60 metres, the standard four-foot target is used, but each colour is divided into two zones. At 50 and 30 metres the target is 80 cms. in diameter in standard colours, and again each colour is divided into two zones.

Before the round is started it is usual to allow six arrows to be shot which are not scored, and these are known as 'sighters'. During the shooting of these sighters there is usually a good deal of sight altering going on as the archers try to compensate for the particular weather conditions of the day.

The usefulness of these rounds is that they enable an archer to compare his scores on a certain round with the scores of other archers and with his own previous scores, and Handicap Tables are available which make it possible to compare the scores of entirely different rounds. (See Appendix). Another good reason for shooting rounds is that they add so much variety to the sport; one week the members of a club can shoot the difficult York round, the next week the less strenuous Western, and so on throughout the year. Many clubs arrange their whole programme for the season at the beginning of the year and put it on the notice-board so that members can decide which rounds they wish to participate in.

During a round each archer shoots six arrows before going to the target to take his score, and this is called an 'end'; but the six are shot in two groups of three, the archers on each target dividing themselves into two sections to shoot their three alternately. Where several archers are shooting together a Field Captain must be appointed who will be responsible for safety. No one must move over the shooting-line towards the targets until the Field Captain has given a signal, usually by means of a whistle, to show that he has checked that everyone has finished shooting; similarly, shooting must not start again after scoring until the Field Captain has given the signal to show he has checked that everyone is back from the targets. Because every club and every tournament sticks to these elementary rules archery is one of the safest sports you can find. If you ever hear someone shout the word 'Fast!' then stop shooting immediately, for this is the archery word for danger.

# Scoring

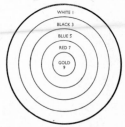

Fig. 24. *The standard four-foot target.*

The four-foot target which is used for rounds is divided into five scoring zones (Fig. 24); the centre circle is the 'Gold', scoring nine points (never call it the 'bull's eye'!), then the Red at seven points, the Blue 5, the Black 3, and the White 1. Because the colours on a F.I.T.A. target are each divided into two zones, the scoring is all the way through from 1 to 10. The exact centre of the target is called the 'pin-hole', and the part of the target face outside of the scoring area is known as the 'petti-coat'.

In charge of each target is the Target Captain, who will take down the scores. Each archer in turn points to the nocks of his arrows whilst the Target Lieutenant calls their value, starting at the highest scoring arrow, and working down to the lowest. It is customary to call them in groups of three to avoid confusion, e.g. 'Nine seven seven (pause), five three miss'. An arrow that is cutting

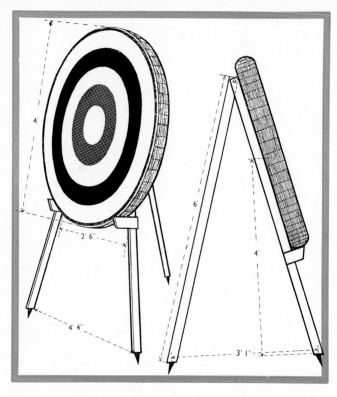

Fig. 25. *Dimensions of target and stand.*

two rings is given the score of the higher value, so if there is any doubt as to whether an arrow is cutting the line or not, the archer does **not** touch the nock or the target face, but instead asks the Target Captain for a decision. At tournaments there will be a judge who can be asked to settle any disputes about scoring.

If an arrow bounces off a target or passes right through, it is not scored, but if it goes through the face of the target and remains sticking out of the straw boss, then the Target Captain removes it and pushes the point back through the boss at the same place and at the same angle until it comes back through the face for a score to be taken. If an arrow hits and remains in an arrow already in the target it takes the score of the struck arrow, but if it hits an arrow already in the target and is deflected **into** the target, it is scored according to its own position. If an arrow is found on the ground and is thought to have struck and rebounded from another arrow, it will be given the same score as the struck arrow provided that the struck arrow shows damage to the nock.

It is as well to mention here that should an archer damage or break another's arrow by carelessness, such as treading on it in the ground he will be expected to pay for it straight away, but any damage sustained by shooting into the target is just the luck of the game.

These are just a few points about scoring, but you would be well advised to buy a copy of the Rules of Shooting (see page 31). Just about every eventuality is covered by these rules and you are sure to find them interesting reading.

# Tournaments

These are simply competitions between archers shooting one of the rounds already mentioned. There are usually a good many prizes to be won, for as well as prizes for the top two or three scores there are also awards for archers of different standards. At many tournaments you will find that besides the difficult York and Hereford there will be a Western, American or National especially for beginners, so do try to get to one as soon as you can. Do not worry about what people will think of you if you shoot badly; they will be far too concerned about what they themselves are doing to worry about you! Tournaments are the most thrilling part of archery, for everyone tries their hardest and the competition is very keen. It is exciting to arrive at the shooting-ground to see the long line of targets already set up, and then to meet the other archers on your allotted target, some of whom may have come long distances for this particular shoot. When the shoot is over and the scores are all collected, the prizes are presented, and the day will come when your name is read out and you will walk up to the prize-table to receive your first award from the Lady Paramount. What an exciting day that will be.

# Other forms of Archery

Target archery is the most popular form of the sport in this country, but a growing number of people are taking up **Field Archery,** which normally takes place in woods and rough fields. Targets of various sizes are used, instead of the standard four-foot one, and they are placed in all sorts of awkward places over a roughly circular course. The target faces are also different, being either black and white circles, or pictures of animals which are sometimes in full colour. No sights are used, nor are the distances of the targets known, for shooting is purely ' instinctive '; in other words, the archer must guess the distance and must also guess where to aim, but with constant practice the field archer can become very accurate indeed.

The anchor is no longer under the chin, but at the side of the face with one of the drawing finger-tips touching the corner of the mouth (Fig. 26). Both the head of the archer and his bow are canted over to the right just a little so that the eyes are over the arrow, and both eyes are kept open to get a better estimate of distance. The archers move around the course in small groups, shooting at each target in turn from marker pegs, taking their scores and retrieving their arrows, and then moving on to the next target. It is tremendous fun, although it can be expensive in arrows to start with.

If you would like to try the type of shooting that was used at the commencement of battles in mediaeval times,

Fig. 26. *The style used in field-shooting.*

for aiming purposes, for the archers shoot from 180 yards (140 yards for ladies), which is much too far to be able to see the rings on the ground. It is almost at the limit of many bows, so the archers are obliged to shoot their arrows high into the air to drop them on to the target, and great attention must be paid to the strength and direction of the wind. It can be very galling to watch your arrows fall directly on to the flag, or so it seems, and then find when you walk down that they are all twenty yards too far or too short!

Slightly similar to this in appearance is **Flight Shooting**, but now the archers are no longer trying to hit a target, they are simply trying to shoot an arrow as far as possible. Considerable skill is needed to shoot an arrow a long way, but also special bows are needed that are designed solely for this purpose, and are never used for any other form of shooting. Advances made in equipment for flight shooting gradually improve the design or materials used in equipment for target shooting, so it is an important branch of the sport.

The style used in field-shooting is also used in **Archery Golf,** which can be a straight match between archers and golfers. The archer's target is a white disc four inches in diameter which is placed on the green next to the cup. For the longer shots ordinary target arrows or even flight arrows are used, but for short distances it is better to use an arrow with a long thin spike instead of the usual point, otherwise when the target is missed by a few

then you must try your hand at **Clout Shooting.** A target 24 foot in diameter is marked out on the ground, and a small flag or white disc is set up in the centre; this is only

inches the arrow may skid on for another thirty or forty yards.

We should not finish talking about variations in shooting without mentioning **Archery Darts.** This is played by archers shooting against an ordinary darts team, but the archers shoot from 13 or 14 yards at a paper face which is marked out as a normal dartboard, but is considerably larger. These faces are quite cheap and are used on a normal four-foot boss. If an arrow should cut a dividing line, then the score is taken according to which side the arrow is nearer, but if the arrow is exactly on the line without bias either way, then it is not scored, for a darts player would have had his dart bounce from the wire.

Apart from this, the game is played exactly as a normal game of darts. It is great fun during the winter to take on the various darts teams in your area, and it is very likely that this will be the means of getting new members for your club. One word of warning; many of your matches will probably take place in small halls or clubs, so it is particularly important that one of your members shall look after the safety aspect and stop people from wandering in front of the target. Many people just do not realise the penetrating power of an arrow.

# Safety

Because the bow is no longer used as a weapon of war people seem to have the idea that it is no longer very dangerous, but of course the use of modern materials has given bows even more penetrating power than the ancient weapons had. An ordinary composite bow for target shooting can penetrate inch thick wood. There is no such thing as a ' toy ' bow; the smallest bow belonging to a child can wound or maim, and an adult's bow can easily kill, so keep this in mind and never play the fool. To aim a ' loaded ' bow at a person ' in fun ' is enough to get you thrown out of a club, and rightly so.

It is foolish to shoot an arrow straight into the air, for even when it is calm near the ground there can be quite strong winds just a few yards up and you never know where the arrow may land. Never shoot an arrow where it may go out of sight, such as over a hill or a hedge; it would be so easy to kill someone. For your own personal safety never use arrows which are too short for you; one may be drawn inside the bow and it will be smashed into flying splinters when you loose. Similarly, it is foolish to repair wooden arrows which have broken, for if the join should break again just as you loose, parts of the arrow may be driven into your hand.

On page 23 you have read that a Field Captain controls the shooting by means of a whistle, and the rule is quite strict. Do not start shooting until the first signal is given, and do not step over the shooting line towards the targets

Fig. 27. *Always keep the bow pointing downwards until the draw.*

before the second signal. If you hear the cry of 'Fast!' you must stop shooting immediately. Archery is one of the safest sports you can find, but only because all archers abide by these commonsense rules.

# Conclusion

Now that you have finished the book you should have a good basic knowledge of archery, and we hope that the fascination of this time-honoured skill has gripped you even more. Archery demands so much concentration to do well that you will find that a day spent shooting will clear your mind of any worries or troubles and leave you pleasantly tired and relaxed, but the actual shooting is not the only pleasurable thing about the sport. There is the enjoyment of making new friends, not just in your own club, but from all over the country as you start to shoot in tournaments. There are the immensely interesting discussions over points of technique, and the long, sad stories of the important arrows that did not go quite right this time. But then again there are those wonderful days when you shoot better than you have ever done before.

In all these things lies the enchantment of archery.

# Glossary

**Anchor.** The position of the drawing hand under the chin.

**Arrow-Rest.** A shelf on the side of the bow which supports the arrow.

**Back.** The surface of the bow away from the string.

**Belly.** The surface of the bow next to the string.

**Best Gold.** The shot nearest to the exact centre of the Gold, for which a prize is usually given at a tournament. It may be judged over the whole shoot, or at one particular end.

**Blunt.** An arrow which has a blunt end or a hard knob instead of a point. It is used for shooting small game.

**Boss.** The straw part of a target without the face.

**Bouncer.** An arrow which has rebounded from the target. No score is given to it, even if a witness saw where it struck.

**Bow-Arm or Bow-Hand.** That which holds the bow.

**Bow Weight.** The poundage required to draw the bow to the full length of the arrow.

**Bow Window.** The gap between the bowstring and the edge of the bow which some archers see when aiming. However, most archers prefer to line up their string with some part of the bow or sight, but without looking through this gap, which can vary in width.

**Bowyer.** One who makes bows.

To **Brace** a bow is to string it.

**Bracer.** A guard made of leather or other firm material which is worn on the forearm of the bow hand to protect it from the string after the loose.

**Bracing Height.** The distance between the bow and the string, taken at the nocking point.

**British Archer.** (The B.A.). The National magazine of archery, published every two months.

**Broadhead.** A spear-shaped arrowhead, used for hunting.

**Butts.** The shooting range.

**Cast.** A general term describing the speed which a particular bow gives to an arrow.

**Clicker.** A device, usually a thin strip of metal, which is fitted to the side of a bow and one end of which rests against the arrow. The archer comes almost to full draw, aims, and when he is satisfied with his aim, completes the draw. As the point of his arrow comes past the clicker, the metal is released to strike the edge of the bow with a sharp ' click ', and the archer then looses. Not for beginners; you've already got enough to think about.

**Cock Feather.** The odd-coloured feather set on the shaft at right angles to the nock. The other two fletchings are called shaft feathers, NOT hen feathers.

**Creeping.** The fault of letting the string come away from the chin during aiming, instead of keeping it pressed in until the moment of loosing.

**Crest or Cresting.** Rings painted around the shaft near the fletchings to identify the owner.

**Draw-Check.** An upright piece of rubber let into the bow handle in front of the arrow rest, which is kept down by the weight of the arrow, but which pops up when the pile is drawn past. It shows the archer that he has reached (and is still at) full draw.

**End.** Six arrows shot consecutively.

**Fast!** A command to stop archers from shooting. It should be instantly obeyed, even when on the very point of loosing.

**Field-Pile.** An arrow point used only in field shooting which is less sharp than one used for target shooting. Should a field archer accidentally hit a tree, the arrow will not embed itself so deeply.

**Fistmele.** A rough bracing height measured with the width of a hand plus the extended thumb. Not accurate enough for modern competition archery.

**F.I.T.A.** Le Federation International de Tir à l'Arc, the International body of the sport, also the round designed by them for international competitions.

**Fletcher.** One who makes arrows, also used to mean one who attaches fletchings to a shaft.

**Follow the String.** Said of a bow which has taken a permanent curve through use. This will happen only to wooden bows.

**Footed Arrow.** A wooden arrow which has the front three or four inches made of a harder wood than the rest of the arrow in order to take the shock of impact better.

**Fru-Fru or Flu-Flu.** An arrow which instead of having three ordinary fletchings, has one full length feather, eight or more inches long, which is glued around the shaft spirally several times just below the nock, so that it looks a little like a sweep's brush. The intention is to stop the arrow from going very far, for the resistance of the fletchings to the air brings it to the ground within 30 or 40 yards. It was invented by the Turks so that they could practise the technique of flight shooting without having to walk long distances to retrieve their arrows.

**G.N.A.S.** The Grand National Archery Society, the ruling body of the sport in the United Kingdom.

**G.M.B.** The title of Grand Master Bowman, the highest standard of archer. Below this is Master Bowman, then 1st, 2nd, and 3rd Class Archer.

**Ground Quiver.** A metal stand placed in the ground to hold spare arrows and the bow when not in use.

**Lady Paramount.** This is the title given to the lady who presents the prizes at the close of a tournament, but she is also in fact the supreme arbitrator in any disputes that may occur.

**Loose.** The act of letting go the drawn bowstring. Archers may loose or shoot arrows, but they never ever ' fire ' them.

**M.B.** Master Bowman, the standard immediately below Grand Master Bowman. Both these titles are also given to lady archers of this standard.

**Nationals, The.** The National Championship of the United Kingdom.

**Nock.** The slots in the tips of a bow, made to take the string, also the slot in the end of an arrow. To 'nock' an arrow is to place it on the string.

**Nocking-Point.** A marked part of the string where the arrow is placed.

**Perfect End.** All six arrows of one end in the Gold.

**Petticoat.** The outside, non-scoring, edge of a target face.

**Pile.** The point of an arrow.

**Pinhole.** The exact centre of a target.

**Popinjay.** A type of shooting where a wooden model of a bird is placed at the top of a mast and blunt arrows are shot at it from directly below. Points are awarded according to which parts of the bird are knocked down. Rarely seen in this country, but popular on the Continent.

**Riser.** The wooden centre of a composite bow from which the handle is fashioned.

**Serving.** A layer of linen thread placed around the centre of the bowstring to prevent the string being worn away by the rubbing of the tab and the bracer.

**Stabilisers.** Metal weights which are attached to the back of some composite bows, above and below the handle. Their purpose is to prevent torque, or the tendency some bows have to twist in the hand slightly when they are loosed.

**Tab.** A piece of leather worn on the drawing hand to protect the fingers from the rubbing of the string.

**Target Day.** That day when a club meets to shoot together a pre-determined round of which the scores will be recorded, as opposed to a day when the archers are only practising.

**Trials, The.** The International Trials, a competition that is held each year to which the best archers in the United Kingdom are invited so that the Selection Committee may choose a team for the World Championships.

**Weight in Hand.** The actual physical weight of a bow, as opposed to the weight needed to pull it.

**Wooden Spoon.** A booby prize, not for the lowest score as one might think, but usually awarded for the worst White at the last end.

Handicap Tables, price 3s. 0d. (please state lady or gentleman) and the G.N.A.S. Rules of Shooting, price 3s. 6d., are available from the Secretary of the G.N.A.S. Please send cash with order; price includes postage.

# Appendix

## GRAND NATIONAL ARCHERY SOCIETY

*Secretary:* J. J. Bray, 20, Broomfield Road, Chelmsford. Essex.

## REGIONAL SECRETARIES

**The Northern Counties Archery Society.** (Chester, Cumberland, Durham, Lancaster, Northumberland, Westmorland, Yorkshire.)
    K. Barnes, Esq., 32 Cambell Road, Winton, Eccles, Lancs.

**The Grand Western Archery Society.** (Cornwall, Devonshire, Dorset, Gloucestershire, Somerset, Wiltshire.)
    R. F. Newton, Esq., Hele Cottage, Old Torrington Road, Barnstaple.

**The Southern Counties Archery Society.** (Bedfordshire, Berkshire, Buckinghamshire, Cambridgeshire, Essex, Hampshire, Hertfordshire, Huntingdon, Kent, London, Middlesex, Norfolk. Oxfordshire, Suffolk, Surrey, Sussex.)
    Miss T. Davison, 102 Ashgrove Road, Goodmayes, Ilford, Essex.

**The East Midlands Archery Society.** (Derbyshire, Leicestershire, Lincolnshire, Northampton (incl. Soke of Peterborough), Nottinghamshire, Rutland.)
    K. Tunnicliff, Esq., 1 Turnfurlong, Northampton.

**The West Midlands Archery Association.** (Herefordshire, Shropshire, Staffordshire, Warwickshire, Worcestershire.)
    Mrs. C. M. Pritchard, 15 Cockermouth Close, Beverley Hills, Leamington Spa, Warwicks.

**The North Wales Archery Society.** (Anglesey, Caernarvonshire, Denbighshire, Flintshire, Merionethshire, Montgomeryshire.)
    J. W. Till, Esq., 16 Mountfield Road, Hawarden, Deeside, Flints.

**The South Wales Archery Association.** (Brecknock, Cardiganshire, Carmarthenshire, Glamorganshire, Monmouthshire, Pembrokeshire, Radnor.)
    D. Mansel-Edwards, Brook Cottage, Lisvane Road, Llanishen, Cardiff.

**The Ulster Archery Association.** (The six counties of Northern Ireland.)
    E. Dougan, 35, Norglen Drive, Belfast 11, N. Ireland.

*National Coaching Organiser:* D. A. Gould, 131, Sandy Lane, Poole, Dorset.